PALLADIUM

ALSO BY ALICE FULTON

Anchors Of Light

Dance Script With Electric Ballerina

PALLADIUM

POEMS BY

ALICE FULTON

THE UNIVERSITY OF ILLINOIS PRESS

URBANA AND CHICAGO

This book is printed on acid-free paper.

Palladium was set in Granjon and Torino Roman typefaces. Book typography and cover design was by Hank De Leo. The cover photograph, a palladium print titled "Woman in the Grass," is by Ellen Foscue Johnson, copyright © 1986.

LIBRARY OF CONGRESS CATALOGING IN PUBLICATION DATA
Fulton, Alice
   Palladium.
   (The National Poetry Series)
   I. Title.   II. Series.
PS3556.U515P3   1986   811'.54   85-31807
ISBN 0-252-01280-1 (alk. paper)

ACKNOWLEDGMENTS

Antioch Review: "Night Gold"
Boston Review: "Aunt Madelyn At The White Sale,"
"Obsessions," "The Wreckage Entrepreneur"
Epoch: "Everyone Knows The World Is Ending"
The Fiddlehead: "Sister Madeleine Pleads For Our Mary"
Helicon Nine: "Fugitive," "Where Are The Stars Pristine"
Hubbub: "All Night Shivering"
Michigan Quarterly Review: "Risk Management"
The New Yorker: "News Of The Occluded Cyclone,"
"Scumbling," "The Ice Storm," "The New Affluence"
Parnassus: "Men's Studies: *Roman De La Rose*"
Ploughshares: "Fables From The Random," "On The Charms
Of Absentee Gardens," "Works On Paper"
Poetry: "Another Troy," "Aviation," "Babies," "Fierce Girl
Playing Hopscotch," "My Second Marriage To My First
Husband," "Nugget And Dust," "Plumbline,"
"The Body Opulent," "Traveling Light"
Primavera: "Mary Studies The Apple Tree"
River Styx: "Days Through Starch And Bluing,"
"The Fortunes Of Aunt Fran"
Sierra Madre Review: "Fictions Of The Feminine:
Quasi-Carnal Creatures From The Cloud Decks of Venus"
South Carolina Review: "Well, Pain's Wildwood Looks Refined"
The Southwest Review: "Peripheral Vision"
Virginia Quarterly Review: "When Bosses Sank Steel Islands"
West Branch: "Semaphores and Hemispheres"
The Yale Review: "603 West Liberty St."

"Terrestrial Magnetism" won the 1984 Consuelo Ford Award from The Poetry Society of America and the 1984 Rainer Maria Rilke Poetry Competition. It first appeared in *New American Poets of the 80's* (Wampeter Press, Green Harbor, Mass., 1984).

I wish to thank The Michigan Society of Fellows, The Fine Arts Work Center in Provincetown, and Cornell University for the support that helped me to write the poems.

I owe special thanks to my mother, Mary Callahan Fulton, for her help with the poems in Part III.

THE NATIONAL POETRY SERIES

The National Poetry Series was established in 1978 to publish five collections of poetry annually through five participating publishers. The manuscripts are selected by five poets of national reputation. Publication is funded by James A. Michener, Edward J. Piszek, The Ford Foundation, The Mobil Foundation, Exxon Corporation, The National Endowment for the Arts, The Friends of the National Poetry Series, and the five publishers—E. P. Dutton, Graywolf Press, William Morrow & Co., Persea Books, and the University of Illinois Press.

The National Poetry Series, 1985

Living Gloves by Lynn Doyle
Selected by Cynthia Macdonald/E. P. Dutton

Local Time by Stephen Dunn
Selected by Dave Smith/William Morrow & Co.

Palladium by Alice Fulton
Selected by Mark Strand/University of Illinois Press

Saints by Reginald Gibbons
Selected by Roland Flint/Persea Books

As Long As You're Happy by Jack Myers
Selected by Seamus Heaney/Graywolf Press

for Hank

CONTENTS

I

II

III

IV

V

VI

I

PA L L A D I U M: (named 1803 by its discoverer, Wollaston, from the newly discovered asteroid *Pallas*): a silver-white, ductile, malleable metallic element that is one of the platinum metals and resembles platinum. It does not tarnish at ordinary temperatures, occurs usually with platinum (as in nickel sulfate and gold ores), and is used in alloys (as with silver) for electrical apparatus and jewelry. Symbol Pd.

> Adapted from the OXFORD ENGLISH DICTIONARY and WEBSTER'S THIRD NEW INTERNATIONAL DICTIONARY

The balance spring is usually of palladium.

> F. J. BRITTEN, WATCH AND CLOCK MANUAL, 1884

The single largest use for palladium is as a catalyst.

> R. B. ROSS, METALLIC MATERIALS

Babies

born gorgeous with nerves, with brains
the pink of silver polish or
jellyfish wafting ornately
through the body below.
An invertebrate cooing
on the mother
tongue shushes and lulls them into thinking
all is well. As they grow they learn

salvage: tear-out
guides to happiness say apologies can outshine
lies, guilt be lickspittled from their lives, bad
glycerined to good. Like a child's first school pencils
in their formal brilliance
and sharp new smells, they lie

as lovers. Maybe one cries
the wrong name and the night skinning
them pleasantly alive
leaps away in shards.
Then it's time for restitution:
a tin of homebaked,
holding gingham safety, fetal
as the light through mason jars of beets and brine,
or jewelry, clasping and unclasping
aisles of fluorescence from great department stores,
a distracting plenitude, and tempting.

Still, the beloved may stay bitter as an ear
the tongue pressed
into, unwanted.
And the word *end:* spiney, finally-formed,
indents them and is
understood. They learn

the hard way as hurts
accrue, and the brain is cratered as a rock
by rain that fell ages past
on unprotected mud. An insult keeps
despite apologies. When it vaporizes at last,
its space fills with grains that harden
to a fossil shaped exactly
like the insult.
They grow up when they know that

sometimes
only a gesture responsive as a heart-
shaped parachute above a jump
a life depends on
to be perfect
the first time will ever do.

Nugget And Dust

My father clipped coupons at the kitchen table,
his numismatic faith burnished like currency
in the safe. He was able
to give himself in visible ways: my birth-
day present, the Buick
Skylark, the silk
he wrapped us in against neuralgia, loyalties
moral as 11th-hour tales
in *True,* the only magazine he took.
Meanwhile, I was full of prim
insurrections, a maximalist
on a shoestring. How could I

admit I withdrew from him
as from a too-gentle thing I wanted to live
forever? I couldn't stand the forthcoming
sadness. Love, if true, is tacit.
It accumulates, nugget and dust, arcade of sweet
exchange. I argued the self-
evidence of all enhancements.
Yet we were camouflaged. I told lies
in order to tell the truth,
something I still do. It was hard

to imagine a world in tune
without his attention
to its bewildering filters, emergency
brakes, without his measured tread. Diligent world,
silly world! where keys turn and idiot lights
signal numinous privations.

Night Gold

We stay up all night and like to
think of others who do: hookers
locking parts in 6 × 10 trash
compacters behind tacit marquees,
night gold traders, aviators
watching jets swoop down, headlights
knighting each shoulder
as they turn.
Everything is louder in the dark, more
seismographic. Certainly
before birth there was no rest
under the earth-
quake of our mothers'
stomachs, and your workaholic throat
muscles dumbly form
these words right now.
We don't hope for a rest-
ful old age, just that
the nonessentials go
first: spare change
when a drunk is rolled.
If we sleep we wake
with marked faces
as if we'd nuzzled
up to lovers in straw
underclothes. By morning our lives
look like bars
stripped of their whiskied
dark: ashy

trappings on display
as the sun, a billspike,
goes through us
and we remember
what we owe
to whom and how
we have to pay.

Orientation Day In Hades

It is not as expected. There is no drama,
no prolix growth of ghostly chains,
just this tin to tie around your waist.
No brimstone, but a mist
rising from the pepper mash
with that pervasive quality
Tabasco has when let loose
in a soup. There is no wind.

Oaks grow in the fields
and are sacred for their shade.
You know trees. They don't suffer
openly. At least you pass the time
with close acquaintances:
bending and inspecting, weeping
crocodile tears in biting air.
Guess you never thought you'd spend forever
as a pepper picker!

And all that talk of bottomless pits
was wrong. It's more a vat,
a barrel slatted with darkness
contained by hoops of energy.
We have a saying: the living die
on a globe, the dead live
in one. But you were close to right
when you pictured this
topography as a stewing

vermilion, the tint
and texture of ground beef.

The courtly, mustachioed fellow
with the military bearing
is, you guessed it, the Old Gentleman
himself. On the sabbath he changes
to an ex-marine in full-dress uniform.
And the green shining in the distance
like letters on computer screens—?
those are the Elysium Fields.
Up close they're pretty
as lime Jello wired from within,
pretty as the Emerald City.
Heaven's that blotto yonder,
under digits of sun.
Light always has a point to make
in kingdom come, as in religious pictures
or Disney animation. That paradise

looks like a salt mine
may come as a surprise. In fact,
it's actually made of salt,
all grayish hills and gooey lights,
as if seen through Vaseline. Rumor has it
some transubstantiation—don't ask me which—
distills human juices, tears and such,
into Zion's saline caves. The Extramundane Union
Tombstone Cutters handle all construction,
which explains the graveyard look.

Angels roost together
like egrets on the salty gates at dusk.

Ages ago I saw one fall.
There was a rolling explosion
as she landed like a cross
between a wind-driven sculpture
and a laden clothesline at my feet.
Her hair had a smell I remember—
cotton candy!

If you look closely you'll catch a glimmer
of the alligator emblem at the entrance.
Of course, we have our jokes
about designer labels, the Izod gates.
They claim reptiles are the sign
of evolution and redemption,
though in my opinion, they picked the loathsome
things to make the blessed feel more holy.
Crocs and gators are just concepts in nirvana land.
The actual critters live down here.
Their long, complacent grins make them
fall short of being so ugly
they're adorable. By rights, they should be

our symbol. They're like everything in Hades—
almost okay. Take the food.
At first it was like living on thistles,
but now I almost relish the tongue-puncturing
culinary voodoo of each dish.
Free will comes down to meaning
we can eat anything with hot sauce on it.
Things are permanently crooked,
out of kilter, whack, on the fritz and blink,
as if seen through the tilt of fever
or new prescription lenses. Perdition's
dizzying. And no one draws the blinds. Heaven's

more formal, a white tie affair,
full of acceptance
speeches in a language sibilant
as something large and tired sinking
to a bed of straw.
Our banter, in contrast, clanks
like cashboxes slamming closed.

But we have a common interest:
Earth's evangelical networks
keep us all in stitches.
"Trade Shows for God,"
that's what we call religion.
The ashtrays shaped like pentecostal flames,
the thousands kissing TV screens
as "the holy beamer" ordains another station,
cathedrals of potluck
praise, where ministers in jargon
suits hold vigils for arthritic miracles . . .
Talk about your jogtrot notions
of infinity! I could tell them

about the bower of bliss
and its flipside. Friend,
you're in the best place
you'll ever be, I'd say.
The arms of the faithful rise, weightless,
as preachers entreat them to
grasp God's celestial hand-
kerchief and hallelujah. To me they look like victims
of a holdup being frisked.
Their prayers waft by, a sticky vegetative flora.
Our oak trees are shawled with the stuff—
you might have thought it Spanish moss.

Now gospel music—a furious condiment
bottled in a body, canned fire backed by choruses
that multiply like viruses
on the words "Temptation" or "Satan,"
ascending to yells elemental
as palladium on "Saved"—
well, those singers have a feeling
for hereafter. They give you hell
and heaven in a nutshell.

On the whole, however, the lamentation
of the damned has been exaggerated.
At night we pickers soak our hands
to cool the burn. We *do* sleep,
and though the peppery fingernails
of horror films claw
through our dreams, we are too tired
to shout and writhe. The only sound's
a suck and splat
as bubbles rise through ripening
ferment.

The Body Opulent

Mr. Silver owned a steel plant
and manipulated auras on the outskirts
of Detroit: a faith healer.
Perhaps he could heal
mine. Through subdivisions trim and brown
as bouillon cubes, defoliated zones,
where heavy machinery depreciated, I took my heart.

The waiting room contained a cloudy sky
made finite in linoleum, a kind of American marble.
Whatever lured me here?
A month ago I'd plunged into a double-dark nothing
like sleep since sleep gives dividends
of dream, free wake-ups. Coming to,
my body less tractable
than a grocery bag of sand,
I knew I'd nearly made the one-stop shopping trip
I'd heard so much about.
Doctors pursued the elusive
verdict, their spooky machines
awhirr with purpose. Their glowing dyes
showed fiery tributaries ribboning
my heart: arabesques of argon violet
crosshatched in patterns so complex
they seemed quite random. It would take some faith
to unravel all that
bafflement! Was it heretical
to expect things from this
world? To want to live

forever in the cells' jewel glut, the body opulent,
a squirming heaven in each fist?

Mr. Silver spoke first of psychics with the power
to bend metal, supernormally
light lamps two miles away,
draw like famous artists, and speed
the growth of seeds. Though he could do none of these,
I sensed a Yankee optimism
when he mentioned his ability to diagnose and treat
disease. "Never mind preachers
finding devils under everybody's skin.
Some things are beyond our knowing.
It's important to believe." When I agreed
he seemed relieved. "All right, sports fans,
let's see if these success stories go beyond
conjecture," he said. I was to close my eyes
and meditate on something pleasant
while he mediated over me.

Though I tried to snag my mind on sweetness,
I kept thinking
this is America. And I hadn't told anyone
where I was going.
He put his hands around my neck and squeezed.
Each cell got busy, singing
the dawnsong of its name;
my body suddenly felt worth its weight
in light, as if I held the sky
above an earthquake—the magenta glow
made by electric fields and shifting
plates—inside each artery and vein.
After thirty minutes he backed off
to give the news. "It's true, you have a cardiac

screw loose. But I'll tell you what
to do. *Smile.* Meditate
like you did tonight. Remember
you don't have to kiss anybody's fanny.
You're going to be all right."
By way of farewell, blessing, or epiphany,
he feelingly recited Kipling's "If."
Then his flashlight led me through a maze
of cold rolled metal, polychromed partitions.

Outside, the night was laced with bright fillips
of pidgin English: Glassbenders,
in bins among transformers, standing
burners, the din and smell of lightning,
formed these Lifesavers and double helices of neon,
an old-fashioned, hard to stack, quickly cracking
stuff. They vacuumed each tube of impurities, primed
the inside with hot-colored phosphor, painted
the spaces between letters black. They burned
themselves welding adrenaline messages
into night: "La Chambre: Exotic
Dancers," "Warsaw Foot-Long." "Elijah's

Hellenic Den" looked the most respectable.
When I opened the door a waiter raised a platter
of flames. "Opa!" the patrons roared
as if their lungs were made of silk
wrapped round a shout.
Still hoping for signs and wonders,
I thought it might mean Health or Life, an omen
of survival. "It's just something we say.
It means like olé. It don't mean
nothing," the waiter told me.
The appetizers were dark and shiny; the wine local,

from grapes grown in the Motor
City, going by its nose of Pennzoil and Prestone.
A dubious sustenance. Yet I swallowed it
like gospel that somehow did me good.
I was lucky, then,

under the enormous torque
of midwest sky, to find my Nova
in the lot, to drive past emblems
galvanizing night: the golden arches,
spirals, labyrinths, and flags; the logos
placed like halos
above service stations—Mobil,
Gulf, and Shell; the freeway's glowing
dot and dash, a path
of crumbs to follow home.

603 West Liberty St.

Captivity is Consciousness.
So's Liberty.
—EMILY DICKINSON, poem 384

They said here, take this,
and I was handed Faith like shelter, food, matter-

of-factly. I learned
about Sin: a tarry fetish, a binge, the devil's stretch

limo, turbine
of desire; and Penance: the bargain

struck, the scrub of absolution through murmurous
screens; indulgence and the State of Grace

entered then: its starry promise, divine
parole select as sterling. Frisked

of aberrations I felt insipid—
a dimestore creche. Evidently the soul

flickered like a flimsy version of the body:
born whole, then fractured

by venial, mortal flaws. I wondered why I lived
in warmth and weight

unlike the air. I touched
myself, tentative, and questioned

futures inlaid with *forever*. At best I could believe
in the quantum world's array of random

without chaos, its multiplicity—a crown
of right responses!—alone seemed moral.

It was faith
like a gate: earthbound, yet

permeable. I could go through.
It was faith, if not exactly

mountain-moving. Not the kind that moves pilgrims
through austere ranges: rumpled

hills in Nepal, the airy gray
of pumice, as if the whole land-

scape levitated. Those pilgrims walk
because they know

the Crystal Mountain is a tent-
pole holding up the heavens. They believe this

because they believe that
100 years ago a white conch shell

fell and a yogi flew on his snow
lion to pierce the capstone, slinging rain-

bows round the clouds. An event
unseen, but taken on

Faith, which is itself in-
visible. It grows in the open

stadiums under mercury
vapors lashed to derricks. It floats

a bristling star above the born-
again, the preacher with one hand raised

to shield or summon. It spins
each soul like a gyroscope and where

it points, we go.

II

P A L L A D I U M: something that affords effectual protection or security: safeguard.

WEBSTER'S THIRD NEW INTERNATIONAL DICTIONARY

The Wreckage Entrepreneur

It takes faith—this tripping through the mixed blessings
of debris with eyes peeled for the toxic
toothpaste green of copper keystones.
On good days Carborundum-bladed saws free sublime
objective blossoms; stained glass
hangs rescued and suspended
like frozen scarves on lines
behind indigents at barrel fires;
granite cherubs wearing crowbar marks
lie abandoned at her door.
After the wrecking ball
she loads her truck with crushed iotas
because cast marble dust's more durable than solid cuts.
Only occasionally, gargoyles blur
under the pressure of her gaze
as if vision were itself corrosive.
Then deco mirrors hold her
as they catacomb the warehouse walls,
and clinging at the empty
gilding of a door, she wants
a shower and lather of pumice
to melt the gritty casing of her
nakedness. How small she looks
beside what she has saved.

When Bosses Sank Steel Islands

in the North Sea, I was issued this survival
suit and hired to dive.
From the chopper I looked into towers
neat as watchworks, fortresses
with orange flares that roared
in gasey, dragonish glamour, with oily steel
stairs whose perforations distantly contained
the sea.

Here wind is unimpeded.
We speak of it in knots,
as if that measure could restrain it.
You have to trust
unsteady things: the sealant, the wet-
suit, the precision of the pressure
chamber. After deep work
I rest for days there, dreaming of sea

level, of leaves, of stone
croft ruins backlit by refinery
lights, rills of yellow
that waver against night like nonpareils or rainbows
in a spill, and black-
backed gulls drilling down
on newborn lambs. Food

and magazines slip through
a lock and music through a pipe. When needed,
a diving bell lowers me to bottom. There

I tend harvest in the dark.
I make sure pipelines
leave the stinger at good angles. I do
odd jobs, cut and join, move
obstacles. Some say a blowout would kill all

those birds with feathery names: the kittiwake, the guillemot,
puffins, murres . . . What can I do?
I know one prayer: send gushers
of sun glad as Boomtowns, send
a breather. I dive to live.
I stand on my survival, a small platform
above the fuel, the revenues. I dive for what
some call a god-
send: Black gold! The world's crude.

Aviation

Nothing is lonelier than what's human: a group of them
at work or play is enough
to send a quiver through
my differences. Especially
up North where windows ignite early,
hanging the dark
with inner lives like tiny drive-in screens
showing underrated grade B stars,
and bingo-playing ladies
hover, intent as air controllers,
above their cards in social halls.
At tables long as football fields, they acquire
a taste for the metallic:
coins, flat Coke; and Bic lighters
puff like the souls of exclamation
points as winners collect
their macrame plant cradles.
I attended once and know
that by the end a gray funk
plaques the air, dense enough to choke a poet
or a pit pony.
But for the cold life you can't do better

than a 6 × 6 mobile hut defined against snow
only by its black trim, like felt-
tip on bond, or lacking trim,
perishing into a blank
square suspended from transmission wires.
Where inside, anglers ease lines through floor-

holes and the river underneath
is gauntleted with hooks to snag tomcod.
By day's end, window ledges bubble
with gleanings: bagged in plastic, the catch
curves like primitive spoons brimful
with a light blurry as the light
through tears. And let me add the certain loneliness

of looking at the snow-
shoe maker: a plump woman in brogues, dark socks,
bifocals, who fixes herself on a frame of ash,
weaving cowhide through its tear-shape.
Who sits, hemmed by maritime
light shed from a window view
of moonish pasture and fishing
boats in their complicated ice-bound
ropes. It takes shoes like blow-ups
of lace, of butterfly veins,
to suspend hunters and lovers
above the delicacies of snow.
I admire her staid aviation
but think she'd have no use for me.
I can tell a snowshoe from a crosse only

because I saw one all-women's match:
the Maliotenam Indian Reserve
versus Ursula's Body Shop.
High colors tussled with the white.
Knowing nothing of the sport,
I was surprised at how important it seemed:
a ball going win or lose
from net to net, flimsy webs
against the shifty air.

Risk Management

Relentless escalators bore us
to this convention where we wander, homogeneous,
sinking into easy chairs
as if our hearts were made of butter. A contained fire

triggered the sprinkler system yesterday.
The burnt sienna plush turned carotene
and I foresaw venture
capitalists huddling in the crawl-
space beneath the smoke, discussing risk
management and right-of-way. Others have slipped

mirrors under doors, dreaming of listening
devices, hush
money, of money
men who speak in megamergers. Dressed in checks

and balances, we the plebiscite
long to rise above the drudge
work, pulp
work, grunt
work and rock out: to ballet, croquet
our days away in light that burns
us to the hidden quick, to be glad
in neon excess
that hits the pavement rippling
as if run through
with a fine-toothed comb.

Still, we've folded classic jackets over
our bodice-ripping
novels: conventions mean accepting as one
thing something that's another
and a different thing. I know

I'd like to astound
the man beside me with a proposition: "What say
we take the next flight to the old world,
visit Lesser-Kvetching-in-Hogsheaven?"
Instead I'm urging the never-impetuous dawn to hurry
with a morning and a plane
that will return me to the place I left. Ten years ago

I stayed up all night chopping vegetables
with denimed men and women to a rock band's beat.
Now in the great arena opposite the lobby
someone watches as 7000 gallons of water churn
with 200 of white paint to lay half
an inch of ice for tomorrow's hockey game.
I'm talking the twin enchantments:

rhythm and precision. At this minute, light from a blast
furnace tigers the foundry
worker's back. His 60-pound ladle swings sure
as an anticipated need. He moves with a ballerina's ease
and strain, allowing us to take comfort in him somewhere
between risk and safety. He's like the convention

of majorettes to lead the Labor
Day parade, zipped in vinyl thigh
boots, suits molten as new pennies
above predictable kicks, batons
that soar, catch the light and twirl
before they're caught.

My Second Marriage To My First Husband

We married for acceptance: to stall the nagging
married friends who wanted us
to do it there and then—
with them. In the downy wedlocked bed
we ask "Is there life after
one-day honeymoons to Kissamee Springs?
Was I all right?" The answers, woefully,
are no and no. And yes,

we lollygagged down the aisle, vowed
to forsake dallying, shilly-shallying, and cleave
only onto one another, to forever romp
in the swampy rumpus
room of our eccentricities: that sanctum
sanctorum where I sport
bedsocks and never rise
till noon. What did we know?
Did you know my love for animals
has always been acute? Perhaps in time
I will become a shepherdess, a jockey.

At the reception every table was adorned
with toilet tissue cy-
cloned into swans. When I unraveled one
to find the charm, the management
was shocked. Dismembering swans!
No bride had ever . . . And the prize, a little gizzard
of a ring, was disappointing. Oh Person,

was it worth it? Of course,
we fit at dinner parties. But as one part warbles
to be normal, another puts a spin on things.
I see you striving to frolic
in your steel-mesh tweeds as I model
chiffon voluptuaries the color of exhaust.

In the wedding album we end or commence
our revels. There we are! doing the cha-cha-cha
to the boom-chick-chick band
in our dyed-to-match togs.
We're getting fat
on the eats, foaming
white crumbs, "Honey" and "Dear"
cumbersome as live doves
on our tongues.

Bring squeezeboxes, gardenias,
a hybrid of the two. Congratulate us,
chums. Smile and freeze: our dimples stiffen
to resolute framed stares. How adult
we look! Our eyes burn
stoplights in the Instamatic squares.

Fables From The Random

TO HANK

As sun tugs earth into an orbit,
fattens apples to red
spheres, as darkness holds
the dyes in cloth or paint keeps
iron assets intact, you preserve, you make fables
from the random.
What breaks without changing

doesn't signify: a china cup
to china chips—that can be
fixed. But paper flaming
to something other
than paper, or the yin-yang
commas in frogs' eggs growing
longer, unrestorable,
alarm the orderly,
the four-four pulse in you.

Threatened expressions settle
at the bottom of your face,
tempting me to chemistry, a science
that locates elements in order
to control them. My mind tips
at every quibble, a scale
capable of weighing hairs.
Have I discovered any comfort?

I learned burning
is a chemical change
and that I'd rather see
the trees take a powder, the sun
give me the slip,
than see the last of you
and your insistent rejection
of what is
and shouldn't be.
Seeker of agendas
hid in astigmatic

mayhem, I need you.
When I tossed bouquets through the open
window of your high and empty room,
some weedy flowers drifting
on the bed, some dangling
from the sill,
you returned to wonder
how I'd managed without a key—
the daisies were so sweetly placed.

Well, Pain's Wildwood Looks Refined:

a decorous everglades. And ill,
a little twister, a wasp's nest's
diligent swarm: Lord Pain. Its music, bad oboes,
calliopes fueling the Silver Flash,
the Whip, the Tilt-A-Whirl, that is the bed
with its chipped grab bars. God help us

to solariums where acoustic shadows aren't
droning keep the sunny side up, up. Give us
framed fabric edens on the waiting room walls,
the shawleries of morphine, Lourdes waters, a warm glogg
of blood in our veins. That's praying.

Try science—where hearts move
by gamma camera, old umbilical
cords make cripples more nimble and hyper-
ventilating in bags wards off
migraines. Breathing and re-breathing:

it's what we're best at. And what if
some wild octopus of the deep
comes or a big black whale or beastie
comes hellbent on gobbling us up?
Then when vespers, penicillin fail,
we'll take potluck, say please, rock me, rock
me in who cares what cold cradle.

Everyone Knows The World Is Ending

Everyone knows the world is ending.
Everyone always thought so, yet
here's the world. Where fundamentalists flick slideshows
in darkened gyms, flash endtime mess-
ages of bliss, tribulation
through the trembling bleachers: Christ will come
by satellite TV, bearing millennial weather
before plagues of false prophets and real locusts
botch the cosmic climate—which ecologists predict
is already withering from the green-
house effect as fossil fuels seal in
the sun's heat and acid rains
give lakes the cyanotic blues.

When talk turns this way, my mother speaks in memories,
each thought a focused mote in the apocalypse's
iridescent fizz. She is trying to restore a world
to glory, but the facts shift with each telling
of her probable gospel. Some stories have been
trinkets in my mind since childhood, yet what clings is not
how she couldn't go near the sink
for months without tears when her mother died,
or how she feared she wouldn't get her own
beribboned kindergarten chair, but the grief
in the skull like radium
in lead, and the visible dumb love like water
in crystal, at one with what holds it. The triumph

of worlds beyond words. Memory entices because ending is
its antonym. We're here to learn
the earth by heart and everything is crying
mind me, mind me! Yet the brain selects and shimmers
to a hand on skin while numbing the constant
stroke of clothes. Thoughts frame and flash
before the dark snaps back: The dress with lace tiers
she adored and the girl with one just like it,
the night she woke to see my father
walk down the drive and the second she remembered
he had died. So long as we keep chanting the words
those worlds will live, but just
so long, so long, so long. Each instant waves
through our nature and is nothing.
But in the love, the grief, under and above
the mother tongue, a permanence
hums: the steady mysterious
the coherent starlight.

III

P A L L A D I U M: a name given to music halls that featured variety bills, revues, pantomime, and plays.

Sister Madeleine Pleads For Our Mary

Dear Sister Immaculata,
Praying that all are well, I write
to request courtesy at St. Peter's
the night of April 4th, 1921, for Sister
Germaine and myself. We shall not trouble you
for meals but dine upon the abundant

nourishment provided by my sister-
in-law, Katey Callahan. You may remember her
daughter Mary as the child who came to school
with a bloody tongue and frightened Sister
Leontine last month. If so, you may recall

that Mary babbled to you of choir voices
melting, white dresses, candy-colored
wreaths and so on, in an attempt to express
her wish to crown the Blessed
Virgin during the May procession, an honor
which, she tells me, you rightly reserve
for the student with the highest grades
in religion. I understand that

our Mary is not convent-ripe, yet
feel sure the years will instill
the decorum we strive to cultivate
in all our Catholic girls, no matter how
deep an affinity she now exhibits
for the fabulous, and the stained
glass, incense, altar linens, twittering

vigil lights, statues, and Bishop's
ring to kiss will one day cease
to make her giddy. God, that Chiseler

of Souls for Paradise, is at work
in her excitement. She is, dear
Sister, struck dumb by the glow
of the Monstrance. Copious
are the questions she's posed
about devotion (fanciful, yet heartfelt,
I could tell): from how we open doors
without a squeak of hinge, walk
with grounded eyes and never run
some innocent wayfarer down, keep
our spines "straight as stickpins,"
an inch from every chair's back,
to the absence of chocolate
malted milk spots on our missals!
High-spirited, yes, a chatterbox,
perhaps, but unholy never; never

truly bold is Mary. During my last meal
with the family, I said "Well, well,
Niece Mary, how do you like school?"
(In answer, a cracked tongue protruded. The minx!)
"Horrid? Well, cheer up. You are only at the bottom
of the ladder, as yet." Whereupon
she said, "Sister, how do you chew with those bandages
around your chin?" (and would continue
despite her mother's "Shush!") "I'm afraid
you'll choke. I lose my appetite."
You see, our very *habits* make her shiver

with concern. "And how did you injure
your tongue?" I inquired. "I skinned it
licking an icey railing then was scared
to go to school and stood outside
an hour in a drift." "I suppose
you were all over chilblains. Am I right?
Heigh-ho! That's a schoolgirl's life. We go to learn
to put up with things. We must work
at pleasing God." Indeed

(and I recount this solely to show the extent
of her reverence) late that night,
when I had occasion to visit the lavatory,
our Mary entered and in the dark
and half asleep unwittingly she
sat on me. Her terrible screams
would have seemed unnatural had I not known her
to suppose we nuns had no bodily functions.

Her mother (who often salts her observations
with a delicious humor) had previously told me
of the little soul's first trip to Mass.
"Let's sit behind this row of coatracks,"
Katey said, pointing to a pew
of Sisters. (Ah well! We must smile
at ourselves.) Whence Mary exclaimed, "Mother,
there's a lady in every one." Many would disagree
but I contend that our divine M.C.
who holds the patent on mirth
would laugh most heartily at this
whimsy. The saints were funny
people, too!

In closing, I do hope that our Mary will be allowed
to celebrate, as Flower Girl, the Queenship
of the Virgin, her highest model,
to whom she is linked by name, and,
as is every woman, by gender.
For until Mary appeared on earth
what was woman? We are now allowed
to take orders and embrace sacrifice
as proof of love. All this we owe to Mary!

When her mother spoke of the cost, I said
"Katey, the very house in which our Lady was born
and in which the incarnation took
place was transported
by angels from Palestine to Italy. The world, as such,
is coming to rack and ruin, as we know
from the Lord himself. Yet He who accomplished that
feat will supply our Mary with dress and flowers."
I further suggested that Katey importune
Mrs. Pierce, for whom she does light housework,
to share the bounty of her garden and closet
and to lend a basket. It can't be denied

that our Mary likes the limelight
well enough, but I have given
her a Scapular for the Propagation
of the Faith which I pray she will wear
in good health as it is a sure sign
of predestination. Please believe
I have no desire to sway you, Sister. I write only
to confide Mary's true worth, promote her welfare,
and apologize for her
tendency to whistle during prayers.
Devotedly in Christ, Sister Madeleine.

Days Through Starch And Bluing

IN MEMORIAM: CATHERINE CALLAHAN, "KATEY,"
MY GRANDMOTHER

Mondays, sweating the flat smell
of boiled cloth, Octagon soap,
washday moves in. Stirring work-
clothes with a stick,
chafing grime against the washboard's crimp,
labor-splurging to coddle the particular
Mrs. Westover's preference for blue and white paper-
ruled pinafores done just so, she knots
cubes of Rickett's bluing in small
knapsacks, swirls them through rinse water
till the tub mirrors a periwinkle
sky for her dingy whites.

Steam and lye.
The wringer chews things dry.

Collars and cuffs are dipped in the hot
icing of starch: crisp wings, crackable
as willowware. She tacks the scrapping
armfuls on five lines: shirts, bloomers,
livelier than when worn,
doubledare the wind. They'll freeze soon enough—
her fingers are stiff as clothespins.
She sings. The sound forms quick clouds
that mark the time: "Take me out to the ball-
game, take me out to the . . ." After dark, she'll drag in
the tough sheets. They'll score the snow toward home.

Tuesdays, uncurling linens,
towel-rolled, water-sprinkled
for slick ironing, she'll iron. Now she counts
her kids back from school. In the kitchen
they're spilling tea on their dresses.
Goodwhite, Proudblue. This happened
every week. She sits to think
of tonight's dinner. Tomorrow's pressing.

Plumbline

IN MEMORIAM: JOHN CALLAHAN, MY GRANDFATHER

The world could snore, wrangle, or tear
itself to atoms while Papa sat
unnettled, bashful, his brain
a lathe smoothing thoughts civil
above fingers laced and pink

as baby booties; Papa, who said of any gambler,
roughneck, drunkard, just "I don't think much
of him," and in stiff denims
toted his lunchpail's spuds
down a plumbline of twelve-hour shifts:

farmed, lumbered, and cow-kicked,
let the bones knit their own
rivet, oiled big wheels that bullied
water uphill, drank stout, touched animals only
unawkwardly, drove four-in-hand, and sired six.

My ideas are dumb: a fizz
mute and thick as the head on a beer
he once thought, who never thought
such clabber could whiz through
genes and seed and speak.

The Fortunes Of Aunt Fran

Whenever I chase the rushhour
bus, Fran returns, in assertive
hat and earrings. Those earrings,
spinning bingo chips
of luck at each lobe,
make my diamond studs
seem tame. I see her turning
collars for eight bucks
a week; I breathe
the cafeteria years.

My aunt had found fast friends
on buses, managed
to love the lumpy banquet
life served up,
out of, I thought, a lack
of hope: that prankster who gooses the humdrum
where it hurts.

And yet, I recall her,
still uniformed,
on our porch, wishing
on the lucky ship,
rubbing its fake
jade hull as the fortune
cookie-Hong-Kong-gift-
shop-tag directed.

Birthdays, she gave
instant lottery stubs:
you got one scrape-
away thrill or millions.
And when young, she'd hop
rides, thumb it, trust her
daredevil luck
before paying busfare. So Fran was

no slouch at being
in hope, in a tryst
that made her spirit
shimmy. She blackbottomed
through The Domino Ballroom
as a girl, tangoed
round the risqué

palladium on Weinbender's Hill
and splurged
her weekly fortune
on eyelash curlers. In photos
she wields a wicked swagger
stick and rat-puffed hair
under a derby.

After school, I'd see her
at the bus stop, humming rock
& roll, rapping
with my friends, admiring
their dashikis and army fatigues.
"Don't Alice look sweet
in khaki green," she'd say.

Her hats heaved higher
as she shrank shorter
and it got harder to see
the person
for the chapeau, though

her natural aplomb
never let the wildest
styles outshine her,
and her self-acceptance was such
that she once asked
the dentist to make her
false buck teeth.

She ferried trays
through the kitchens of Troy
High and The Daughters
of Sarah seven out of seven
days; that's why
I think of her
whenever I'm in motion. "Fran

you had chutzpah," someone said at her
wake. And emblazoned with that
Yiddish praise, she bobs through
my mind like a dingy, riding out
jinxes, ill winds, and tidal waves.

Aunt Madelyn At The White Sale

Here in the kingdom of irregulars,
land of no-two-alike,
I hunt furiously
useful towels. Closets simmering with
terry, linen, beach or tea
can never be full
enough to stop these sprees.

Hoarding is relative
to love or fear, but not to need. Mother stockpiled
soap in step-on cans.
When the lid snapped back,
instead of grinds, grease, skins, it was good
to get a whiff
of the bars, neat and brightly wrapped as gifts.

Waving us off on dates, she'd yell "Be back by twelve
and don't come home
if you get killed." But I wasn't killed,
easy as that seemed. I hadn't figured on
life's pigheadedness:
how the breath and pulse are triggered by a hardwon
inability to unexist. How death is

tightfisted. I thought
at first there'd been a car crash: my voice soared, brilliant
and bubbling with drugs: oh, that that too too
euphoric
stutter should be mine!

Then, with a coziness worse than constraint, they
spoke of the cerebral pinch I'd been in, praised

the luck that chucked me
back to sanitized light. Where towels absorb their weight
in chaos. Where I am serene.
Like those damn orchids—
vivid, blizzardy sprays Tom and I trucked
out West that time, and, one by one, heat or dark
got them: my brainwaves.

The last was that dendrobium . . . or is
that my medication? See? Last week I went
and rang the wrong bell
after twenty-odd years of visiting
my beaming, well-meaning sister.
I worry now
about another sister who manages neither

smiles nor meaning. Those years I coaxed her through
treatments, hoping—
if not for her thanks or love, then what?
Nothing . . . but the nothing I've received
has me shuddering.
Rage makes my blood astringent as witch hazel.
I'll pretend not to see them pretend not to

see my infirmities:
My restless hands. Idling. Pilling the spread.
Of course, you can get killed at home and that's something
Mother never mentioned. My mind drifts
to my friend Miriam, that deadly fire—I see again
her pleasant, stocky face. "Mada, we're sharp
as ever," she said last time,

but she was fooled. With luck she slept right through.
Outside snowflakes lift, float sideways, and seem
to say "ground has nothing
to do with me!" But this is silly.
Though I can't trace one among the calm bustle
of shoppers, I tell myself
they *are* falling, they *do* touch earth, and they

never rise at all.

Mary Studies The Apple Tree

Scanty, white as undies, she
forks through the hedge, tweaking
its decent green geometry. Sun licks
the juices up and into
her buds she springs petals. Now limp with years
I study her rugged curtsy.

Once Mother tallied six kinds of apples on her—
from pink meats, gingery
as grass, to green, water-smelling ones.
Legs kneading air, I swung high,
scouting miles of clothesline basting house to yard,
and touched a burning apple with my toe.

When lightning jumped the parlor's dark
we heard a long-drawn crash of apples
that spiced the ground, snarled
the lines with branch, and trimmed to stump,
only her roots still pumped tough jubilees—
sixteen blooms, all different, I counted recently.

IV

PALLADIUM PROCESS: a contact photographic printing process similar to the platinum process except that a palladium salt is used instead of a platinum salt for coating the paper.

Adapted from WEBSTER'S THIRD NEW INTERNATIONAL DICTIONARY

Both platinum and palladium produced prints with beautiful rich blacks unobtainable with silver. The great advantage of the process was that the image was permanent.

Owing to the scarcity and high cost of the basic materials, these processes have gone out of use.

THE FOCAL ENCYCLOPEDIA OF PHOTOGRAPHY

Whenever possible I use sunlight to print. Because of many variables in paper, chemistry, procedure, and even weather, it is all but impossible to achieve two prints from the same negative that look exactly alike. Therefore, many of these palladium prints may be considered to be one-of-a-kind images.

GISELA GAMPER, photographer

The Ice Storm

It's a world stiff as a principle:
glitter drills both retinas at a glance,
as if the pupils were forced wide
by dilation drops: militant
                  yet democratic, ice built this
superstructure of light, flinging
beaded shawls around the meanest shrubs,
tinting shadows a catatonic mauve,
making weeds brittle as invalids'
glass straws. Overnight, ice struck
rainbows in the dung. The world's become a vision
                of the needles and pins that spark
across restricted limbs: the trees creak
like a crop of dreary
windchimes or glow like frazzled
candelabra under sunsets
marbled as sirloin.
                Now tract housing's polished
to the sheen of citadels,
the hack horse looks unbalanced
in the blinding yard, and pheasants leave
red beads when they tear
themselves to air:
a red less desultory than the gemmy
flashes that resolve
themselves to trees,
                heretic as the heart's red
breaking, through extravagant beats,
the etiquette of ice.

The New Affluence

Let me say "we" for I am not alone in this
desire to live
where the land is neither dramatically flat
nor high, where it snows enough
to keep the world
the bitter white of aspirin.

People with such needs grew up
snow-belted, rust-belted,
in towns like mine, where muscle
cars dragged down Main Streets
and the fountain's aigrettes outside
the Miss Troy Diner offered welcome
hits of pink and blue in a landscape
largely the noncolor of lard.

Our choice: to love or hate
the slight reprieves from plainness: the fractious birds,
the scrappy trees, and most of all
the things that didn't live or breathe—
factories tearing up the sky with smoke,
tugboats sweet as toys
along the poisoned river.
A budget, if not famine, our lives.
Perhaps a sweepstakes, with prizes so slight
no one cared to enter. We wouldn't have become
susceptible to the tag ends, seconds,
as-is of experience, given better

scenery. We wouldn't have gotten this idea
that happiness is mined like ore from rock,
through efforts of imagination. We, the poor,
but not in spirit, we
the not especially blessed,
who, working cold hours at dull jobs,
drank, gambled, went mad, or grew
anomalous as water—
a compound that expands while freezing.

Disciples of steam and dust,
we take pleasure in considering
the glaciers beginning
in the clouds, the picnic springing up
around the subatomic
particles others call the vacuum.
Our sensory thresholds—the nerve centers
that decide what to let us know—let us know
too much, which makes us terrible
at parties: we seize upon the slight
conflicting tics in idle chitchat,
the wayward rift behind a smile.
It's exhausting, and a social hindrance.
Twitchers, fainters, cringelings,

I'm here to say you'd like it
where I live. In this converted bakery
everything's left to the imagination:
the golden smell of molten sugar, the customers
gazing at pastries baked from scratch
into planes and turrets
fanciful as women's hats.
A tub of lard, sealed and dated 1900,

was the one remaining trace
of baking and we left it
sealed, imagining a cache
of rancid snow within.
The local paper gives advice to liven up our days:
"Colored towels add eye-spice. Look for cotton
run-on sales. A blub-blub of vinegar
adds zip to many dishes. Try it, it's terrif."

It was the absence of spectacular views that made us
see the sparrow hopping warily,
as if the ground were strewn with acid.
(Medieval legend says it hissed
"He lives," to Roman soldiers at Calvary,
for which God bound its feet forever
with supernatural string.)
Lacking diversions, we've turned furtive
in order to observe it. We toss crumbs
while light pours crisp as seltzer, as peppermint
oil through air.

The hyacinths need these cold weeks
to grow into fragrant vases
full only of themselves, their particular
being, like everything else.
So summer comes
to meet us. Soon children
will sell chances on rocks and leaves
from sidewalk stands.
Children! They think these things
are valuable. And we always buy.

Fugitive

Stars, though famous
by definition, are anonymous
in spirit. Unlike boys,
the star did not demand
a certain level of response.
She could flip
through rows of him without feeling
blunt. She imagined that he imagined her
and that was how she could exist.
Like a captive crisscrossed
from room to room across a nation,
she had trouble telling
one place from another.
For instance, she believed the same class
had been going on for years
throughout her school.
Priests were mixed messages; their words
formed a gray frost
on her face like breath on a wind-
shield. "You haven't
a chance," they seemed to say.
"So take it." In their black
casques, most of the sisters
listened like women who had been
killed several times. Nones,
she thought. In class
she wished up gardens
off the straight and narrow
toward water events, stone holes

spouting, cherry trees
that drew things
to them and disposed of them.
A mildly active perfection: hundreds of goldfish
flitting like polished nails
in ponds. Or a mossy house
with walls of water—so risky
no one would stay for long.
The days were held
breaths let out
with irritation when she got home,
as if someone there had clamped
a hand over her mouth.
At night she clipped
articles about the star
and read. Books understood her. She read
how you could lose
a limb and still feel it
reaching. But her experience was, as ever,
opposite: you could keep a body and feel
you'd lost it. She had
long nails and always did
everything with them.
But to play the star's
songs on guitar she had to
clip the white tips.
The strings left pink
incisions backed by fugitive
stings, surprising
after years of not touching. She began to dream
the auditory dreams
of the blind, to read in the dark
and with her hands, like them.

Scumbling

Absolved, face to the wall, alive only
in fact. It was always evening
in my head, an evening of thoughts
cool as sheets. His skin
made its silk sound, no
two glissandos alike. A fine fear
streaked through. Let somebody else
sponge up those tremors.
My reserve circled, imperial
as the inside of a pearl. All night
I pretended night was an unruly
day. I pretended
my voice. I pretended my hair. I pretended
my friend. But there it was—"I"—
I couldn't get rid of that.
What could I do but let it learn
to tremble? So I watched feelings hover
over like the undersides
of waterlilies: long serpentines
topped by nervous almost-
sunny undulations. I had to learn
largo. I had to trust
that two bodies scumbling
could soften
one another. I had to
let myself be gone
through, do it in the arbitrary light
tipping and flirting
with seldom-seen surfaces.

Palladium Process

I, a cloud
chamber. My face, a flag-
stone over feeling: if touched I knew
the indentation would fill slowly
as a hole in sand. I was islanded,
a nightingale that couldn't sing
while anybody watched, caged
in paper screens emitting a faint light,
the view through a glassine, scarcely
glanceable. Each day became a vacant lot
I trimmed with safety
scissors, blade by blade. Skirted, stalled,
in the realm between feeling and expression,
sensations fell to me as stones fall
down a well: the wait, the distant clink.
Joy, too, sank: sand in an hourglass,
gravity-tamped.
                        Yet the mystery simmered:
love and rage dried and piled up
like hay in stables that combusts
in tongues. It took angers, lovers,
to enfranchise me. There was this difficult rip-
cord! Then control scattered
as I edged toward expansion.
                        When I came to life
as to a come-as-you-are
fiesta, wrongly dressed, my face
had the telltale patina of solitude,
the strangeness of statues

dragged from sunken holds.
And my happiness seemed silly
as a terrier's in a blizzard, chasing
every dizzy flake.
                    At last, the world surprised me:
I became a student
of surplus, moved by the ubiquitous, sometimes
broken roses, or the serious
hilarity of the stars. I started
at ordinary things
the way a 19th-century gentleman might
start at a glimpse of undraped
limb. Shivers. There were
dictionaries. There were tricks
of the light, dextrous
evanescent cathedrals, improvident
constructions, inventories
like the palladium inventories of
sun!

Works On Paper

A thrilling wilderness of bio-
morphic script, you said
my letters scared you. And it's even worse
in person: pink oil of lipprints, unnervingly organic
Hi's, those kisses like collusions. For a moment
we vibrate like underwater stones.
What is this
windfall? We are not easily becalmed.
How you pull back
as if to deflect affection.
How I pull back, swear
to clothe myself
in jokes. Graft the properties of blandness

to the social handshake
and we'll have it: how to get through
this world intact. Placebos do
nicely—expressions never point
blank but fixed
like bets between grin and grimace.
What I work to know is whether passion,
roaring, snapping
its head, can be prelude
to entertainment, harmless as MGM's
old lion. And is seduction a science
or a pattern of cheap frills; can you make it
from a kit? What suave

impoverishments we chose.
And I can do it: fake

formality, dissemble
with the best, lady it
over lessers: Pick me!
Pick me! Of course not
to care, to keep
the heart complacent as a dumpling,
that's hard. What of emotions
that grow so steep they can't hold
shape and the pinnacle
leaps forward, breaking as it does
in waves? I'm afraid

those emotions keep us lonely.
I'm afraid there are no bribes
equal to the body-
guards. We love surface
articulation. And when we say
Abandon abandon we mean it
as a command. Here's an illustrative touch:

Delacroix, old realist, got so excited
entering a harem's room
he had to be calmed
down with sherbets. Passion! Maybe
it only works on paper. But once
in a well-lit room
I buried my face in the material,
shirting, that opened to darker emulsions, rich
scents unlike others as burnt umber's
unlike other colors. It was about expansion.
There were brief constellations
down the willing nerves,
an effulgence: worth it, worth it.

Peripheral Vision

FOR DAVID LEHMAN

The window's a slow-moving liquid.
In it, the scientist sees another window
drifting: smaller,
larger, smaller. It is the opposite
structure rocking, or her own
structure or herself. Her colleagues watch

a film of their last field
trip. She's distracted
by their black and white extremities,
the ancillary hands and feet. What blooms
beneath their suits, snug
as guilt? Snug as God
in a hideaway heaven, chanting
standard tasks: observe, examine,
isolate.

The screen's a jungle.
On it, others study flirtatious affidavits:
the jeep's tracks mixed with the tiger's
four-toed flash.
They funnel white cloth
between trees, knowing a gauntlet
strongly felt but faintly

seen will spook the tiger
to the darts, the collar
with its battery-
driven signal. Once they have it

ticking, aerial tracking
charts its drift, antennas
on each wing
strut sounding loudest
when pointed toward kinetic
yellow. After canvasing negative space
for ages, the trackers should grow
eyes on stalks that fan the air and fasten
like stays to their domain. Seeing's

such a commemorative gesture. The scientist focuses
on the fiery valentine
that is the tiger's nose.
Is there a cover equal to the giveaway
signal? Does the thought admit regret,
resistance? The heart's a partisan,

but intellect, a stickler, wants to know
in what sense precisely
the tiger's burning bright.
The heart envisions God
in Greece, blasting gilt
from acroliths, exposing
wooden torsos belied by marble arms.
But the mind insists
the God of triangles would be
three-sided: we see what we want
to see. She knows that

glass is a skittery solid,
and film a chain of static frames,
that nature is unchanging,
though it does change. Driving
home, sun slices, horizontally, a line

of trees, or trees skate
past the rooted sun, or cars drift
by the steadfast sun and trees.
What will it be? When God is a round
centered everywhere,
a circumference found nowhere, expanding
the universe, building

new alloys from happenstance and junk.
So constancy won't hold
her. The pupil's noose fits
mornings shaped by matchstick
blinds, the dawn cracked into
even lines. But vision twists
galaxies through the window,

holistic. Her mind works
toward the marginal,
what's tentative but ready
to take on sound and color: the radio tower
underwired with subtle
stripes and flames, invisible leapaway
music bulleting to distant hit parades.

V

PALLADIUM: in classical mythology, a legless image carrying a spear in one hand and distaff and spindle in the other. Athena made the palladium in memory of her childhood playmate Pallas. As girls, the two practiced warlike games together, and during such friendly combat, Athena accidentally killed Pallas. (Later she added her murdered friend's name to her own.) The goddess had also killed a giant named Pallas, and she used his tough skin as a shield. This shield, known as the aegis, she wrapped around the breast of the palladium.

Adapted from EDWARD TRIPP: CROWELL'S HANDBOOK OF CLASSICAL MYTHOLOGY

Palladium also means a stone or other cult-object around which the girls of a particular clan danced . . . or the boys leaped.

Adapted from ROBERT GRAVES: THE GREEK MYTHS: 2

Fierce Girl Playing Hopscotch

You sway like a crane to the tunes of tossed stones.
I am what you made to live in
from what you had: hair matted as kelp, bad schools.

Oh, you will never know me. I wave and you go
on playing in the clouds
boys clap from erasers. I am the pebble
you tossed on the chalked space and war-
danced toward, one-leg two-leg, arms treading air.

In this, your future, waves rechristen the sea
after its tiny jeweled lives
that hiss "Us Us" to the shore all day.
Where's the kid called Kateydid? The moonfaced
Kewpiedoll? The excitable pouting
Zookie? The somber O-Be-Joyful?

Lost girl, playing hopscotch, I will do what you could.
Name of father, son, ghost. Cross my heart and hope.
While the sea's jewels build shells and shells
change to chalk and chalk to loam and gold
wheat grows where oceans teetered.

All Night Shivering

It must have been the cruel age,
when girls shoved open
hands against my chest, crying
"Get a bra!" and Ma wouldn't let me
out till I'd scraped the shame
from my armpits, a black aromatic
penance and having no say-
so, I did
what I was told.

Before entering the theater's private
night, all I knew
of the English had me half-scared
the singers would have teatime
breeding, fustian underclothes.
But when the first one spoke,
his lilt ransacked my heart
like a pandemonious hormone
you can't say no to. Electricity stood
in them like the current in walls, available
whether they sang or not,
and when they sang
their lush drawls enkindled
me on the spot. ("He has a speech
impediment," my killjoy
sister said.) I realized the possibility
of discreet enchantments
under tight pegged pants; salty
princes sent from heaven

with a shout
to let the needy love.

At the end they soared
in a helicopter, dropping letters
that spiraled down like happy accidents
to a 7th chord's hosanna.
The lights came up and I remembered
my best friend in her chubby
anklets and unbecoming jumper.
Our looks confirmed a desire
that was red with impossible
edges and constant.
We soon masterminded a way
to avoid being
ousted between shows.

When the theater closed, we stayed
up all night shivering,
whispering of the men unlike the boys
we knew, with their carlust and girlscorn.
And though we had seen much
that day, we thought
of what we hadn't seen:

Of gravity-defying male
embellishments, wild-smelling
lianas under wraps, long fingers
made for fretwork, and we slept like princesses
above the ticket stubs, the unassailable
proof, bright welcomes
to a blessing, a curse.

Obsessions

steady as the heat
bugs' drone, a rip of white
water too violent
to support much
life. *Only, only, only*
that's the song, self-
absorbed and hardly knowing

us. Meanwhile, our faces vibrate
with desires visible as the inner
workings of certain see-through fish.
How to be more
guarded? Our jaws move
precisely and silk issues
forth in double strands. We speak

in meshes accurate to a ruler's least
degree. Such eloquence, such craft!
Each facet of our fascination
expands. What's desired slips
from its true scale, becomes meta-
physical as a blown-up cell: an opalescence
of congealed light, a shimmering

edema. Blinding.
A close brush with attainment quite
undoes us. We feel
heavily unconscious, submerged in colors dense
as chloroform, distant

effervescent riffles, the roar of boulders in a whirlpool,
slight sandy agitations. If we get near

enough to touch
the desired feels unsettling,
on the fringe of foreign
elements: downy as an algal mat. Sometimes
wanting so unwisely is enough
to make us wish the sheeted surface would break
loose. We'd almost welcome ice

scours, a strict denuding, *only:*
under the numbness, lesser lives
still cling and fight—
one thousand to one
cubic inch. You'd think they counted
themselves dear. You'd think we encouraged
their drowsy, unseen births, breathed on them,

said *treasure.*

Fictions Of The Feminine: Quasi-Carnal Creatures From The Cloud Decks Of Venus

I. THE COCKTAIL WAITRESS

Before work, I practice Bo-Peep put-offs under veils
of Maybelline, pop two No-Doz, and stop
at church. I pray
for the creeps with bucks
to burn, for those receptacles,
the dancers, who throw their legs
over strangers' shoulders, rolling
their heads and tongues in scorn-
ful seizure; pray to escape this low-class pain, become a flight
attendant. Sometimes I'm the only decent female

in the place. A magenta spotlight,
a glitzy reptilian globe, dyes flesh
the winking livid pink
of badly tuned TVs.
Stone freaks, diddlers, Raincoat
Charlies stare at the strut-
way through three-dollar beers
or scan the racked fantasies
in back: ersatz nuns
with bewildered German Shepherds, condoms
stamped with El Greco's
"View of Toledo." Above me,

women spiked with hard-
ware strip down to garters
full of dollars. It gets in my head,
bothers my mind to see
their breasts cemented by silicone, unmoved
whether they laugh or cry, faces so puffy
they have to sleep upright
to keep the stuff from slipping.
I hate them

for the way they hurt themselves, working
this place like a purgatorial
gyno ward, letting hope live
in their smiles like a tic, thinking some Sugar
Daddy will save their lives
in Vegas, a vested broker wive them,
the way Aztec victims thought
they'd go to heaven and be reborn as hummingbirds
or goddamned butterflies.

II. THE PARALYZED CLIENT

To replace thought with sensation, that's why
I come. To see pouty flowers

squirm in mimeo-
violet light, three floors of XX fun.

As a kid, XX stood for kisses:
now, of course, it's different. They swivel down the ramp,

germ-sinuous, diseaseable as
scavenger eels eating up dead

rivers, the swash and backwash
of their strip, their looping moves, powerful

and crass as propaganda. "Showgirls."
What a sham! Only shiftless

idiotheads would work this gig.
I have a certain objectivity. As a kid, I saw

slides of atrophied muscle,
my own, I bet, magnified 1000✕:

gauzy as cheesecloth, a fine plaid lilac.
Dad was a pathologist. I have his

scientific eye. I hate
the other patrons with their static

can-do vanity, hate the haggling
glances of these pancaked tramps.

Last week, blunt as a judge,
one offered me a real sex rub. Took me

for a sucker, another fool
for oogling, but I knew her gaff

game: the knockout
drops in liquor, the stacked

quarters—they'll clip you.
I've ordered a power-

driven chair. Then I'll be able
to travel with the lightning

menace of a centipede, a gladiator
in fetters. I'll come armed

with shellcrackers, live
ammo, do some damage to the situation,

put a stagger in their struts.
As a kid, I'd find human

limbs in the fridge.
I've always been like this.

III. THE STRIPPER

"100 Pounds of Passion
from London's Mousetrap Lounge!"
The histories they invent for me . . .
I'd like to enter shrink-wrapped in lead
sheeting, leopard skin, tinsel, and an orthopedic shoe.
"A Fiction of the Feminine, a Quasi-Carnal Creature
from the Cloud Decks of
Venus," I could be. Elevated
feeling's always rhythmic. I dance
to gutbucket jazz, to fragments of myself hung-
up in mirrors across the room, swiveling
with the current like a body in a river. A good strip
depends on intricate, smooth moves, a thrust for every nut:
the hook and eye
and switch and mince, the wrench
kicks, heavy-duty ratchet
dips, the chops, the hits, each detail planned and weighed
like a successful suicide. At the end I pick up
the moltings, go backstage.
The dressing rooms of skin boutiques smell
haunted—decades of burnt sweat, I guess.
Once, doing breastercises with a pair of brass fire
hose nozzles, I saw this antique spangled tarantella
of a burly queen, showing her fangs
and laughing at me, the flabby old vamp.

Most dancers here are lesbians.
The creeps that patronize are sick. I say
they have fiberfill for minds, icicles for dicks.
They think they're special, though, the dimwits.
When they ask, I say I'm quitting to work with autistic kids.
Some girls go
horizontal, do floorwork,
some clubs have touch, but I never get on
eye level. I make the dumb fucks look
up. Last night they rolled a wheelchair
at me like a bowling ball. "Farther!" he yells,
tears running from his eyes, mouth, nose.
They come to drool
at us marooned in black and white,
in either/or, virgin/whore.
The spotlight, the darkness,
shields them like the polished visors of riot
police. Appetites like this are dangerous, growing
on what they can't quite handle.
But I prefer that to any
vis-à-vis. I'm a modest person by nature.
To tell the truth, I do this now through force
of habit. One night, for a hoot, I'll put pasties,
gown, mask, wig and boa over a rented skeleton suit.
Moving slowly, I'll pose, give
looks, then what a show! I'll come bumping
through their heads stripped down to a string
of glowing bones: the ultimate
in unpeeled flesh.

Men's Studies: *Roman De La Rose*

One inch can make the difference. This they know.
With heads like gaudy jawbreakers
above the platforms of their shoulders,
with fragile penetralia
under guard and balls cupped close, they tumble
into the brine and Ben-Gay of each other's flesh,

into the New Year. The Good Year
blimp, a silver football,
gives insight to the nation.
Here, men float bright as pool
toys through air alive with hail: the weather's
like a slow replay of coiled serrated steel

as it leaps from a grenade. Sports and war
want stripes to stay the flesh.
Mark the saturated solids
ripped by solids primary or secondary
that score their uniforms; the bars of kohl
beneath their eyes.

At the start, both teams are equal,
but the goal's to prove them less
so. How they throw themselves
at themselves, rolling over the curvaceous rose
stained in the grid. A cardinal number
graces every player's chest. Collate,

collate, or the plays decay to random
thermal motion. Now number one has fallen,
and he does not rise.
Through binoculars we watch
the brilliant pom-poms tossing
from his lungs.

The planet earth floats by, a study in the round
of roses, bleeding hearts, and football
mums. At precise intervals,
it opens like a Fabergé egg
upon a hub of coronation gold
and silver lilies turning
half a millimeter per second
(or half a football field
per day) in a bluff of molten flux. "All American"
marigolds arc in and out to sham magnetic action,
and the whole field reverses itself
to "dasher" zinnias at random.

It is the Tournament of Roses floating
down Orange Grove Avenue: The Union
City Golden Tornado Band; cowboys
astride albinos dyed to match
the pink impatiens of their eyes;
100,000 flowers sunk into every float.

Inspired by the theme "Man's Science
and Technology," a watch manufacturer
has launched a fleet of timepieces:
"Jacks-of-the-clock" (all former Miss Pasadenas)
strike the hour with gladiola-plated hammers and a cock

of jacob's rod flaps atop
a rose-encrusted model. Behind it
drifts a clock to gauge the wobble
of the earth's axis over 20,000 years.
All of its components—mainspring, flywheel, even
the escapement at its heart—
are barnacled with early Darwin
tulips. What next, what else? What's left
but a scale model of the world rising
infinitesimally to meet our falling
steps, with all five billion of us on it, crying
Hi Mom, Happy New Year, and waving party hats.

It would be a study in the attraction
between bodies, the subliminal
accommodations nature makes.
But reasons would cheapen
such transient extravagances,
meant to travel at the pace of dreams,
their hardware under wraps of blossoms, blossoms
chanced to sun and hail.

———————————

Defense/offense. Bigger's best. So super
is prefixed to all they do. But to penetrate
their armor is to find them,

in the coiled intimacies
of ganglia and cell, not unlike, in fact,
as intricate, as frail, as roses.

And at the hub, their love and hatred
clenched like buds that die
if opened by forces other

than their own. Later there will be consolations:
wet bars stocked with dry martinis,
8-jet Jacuzzis to make them new.

But first the victors, the Trojans
or Cougars, ritually slap hands. We splash cockades
of champagne on these gainers

and breakers of yards and records,
who believe such measures
prove the better man and play for the gold

we pour, stinging, over the rose
medallions on their shoulders,
over the star-gauged helmets of their skulls.

VI

THE PALLADIUM dropped from the heavens into the city of Troy. Regarded as a guarantee of safety during the Trojan War, it was captured by Odysseus and Diomedes with the help of Helen, and, shortly after, the Greeks were able to conquer the city.

Adapted from EDWARD TRIPP: CROWELL'S HAND-BOOK OF CLASSICAL MYTHOLOGY

When cult objects became identified with tribal prosperity and were carefully guarded against theft or mutilation, palladia was read as meaning *palta,* or "things hurled from heaven."

At first, meteorites, as the only genuine *palta,* were taken to be the origin of lightning. Worship of meteorites was easily extended to ancient monoliths.

Adapted from ROBERT GRAVES: THE GREEK MYTHS: 2

Another Troy

When the Green Island Bridge, a scowling trigonometry of over-
wrought iron from the 1800s, veed
into the river, we danced
all night at a tri-city block party, giving thanks
that none were hurt, and at dawn we printed
tee-shirts, petitioning
that the wreckage be preserved. We loved a ruin.

After dyeing our roots
with toothbrushes from Tek Hughes
on giddy high school Fridays, my friends and I
sauntered in electroplated glory by the river.
Like water lilies wan and local, species Trojan,
condoms bobbed above the current after Happy Hours.
What would the Hudson River School have done
with this? "Troylets,"

so the college students called us,
Trojans being too noble
for makers of Rototillers and shirts.
I, too, felt embarrassed
by Troy's futile boosterism: the schemes to sell itself
as "City of Friendly Service"
or "Home of Uncle Sam" were failures
of imagination. In the seismic hiss of the Volcano

Restaurant I invented Armageddons
guaranteed to free us: fires coasting down from heaven,
spumes of air pollutants hurled into the stratosphere
and we, the *damnificados,* fleeing.

An erupting Italian restaurant—
that would put us on the map!
Evacuated to faraway gyms, we'd picture the cinders,
an eiderdown drawn over dinettes
and reproductions of *The Last
Supper* in our scruffy, buckled homes.
As when the bridge fell, no one would be scratched.
But Troy's rough edges
would be buffed by the crumbled palladium
of ash. A local poet liked this plot

and used it in a sonnet. I starred
as Signorita Mount Saint Helens,
an Irish-American flamenco dancer
burning up the backstage of his heart.
But when I climbed on podiums to scream
in praise of rebels torching
"draft cards, bras, and ghettos,"
the poet refused to speak to me.
If asked I could have told him
that being typecast as the Muse
makes arsonists of women who aren't fools.

In time, I escaped the ruinous romances,
but Troy remains. Today the eccentricity
of its willful brick begins
to look like character.
Oh, if I sing of icicles
dangling like syringes from friezes
"neo-grec" or French,
of roses battened down with sackcloth, trees
lumbagoed under lumpen winters,
I'm minting an insignia. Take this, "Troy—
the City without Glibness,"
for your spartan tribute.

On The Charms Of Absentee Gardens

Let's say the residents had other engagements. They've gone
off playing flutes made from wingbones of the golden eagle.
They've ascended to the abalone heavens, and left
alone, we prettify the long ago.
Aren't gardens most fetching when nobody's home?
When you can track the sunflower's tambourine face
twirling toward the sun.

The Anasazi angled rocks to catch the solstice
sun and show it in the shape of ingots
on a spiral glyph. We need such leavings—
not to tell the seasons but to help us
imagine famine, fire, abandonment. To help us see
catastrophe—the mesa as the basal column of a bomb drop.

Some say remnants of the World
Trade Center will leave much to be desired.
But isn't that a ruin's purpose—to be less
than satisfactory, only partly-
knowable, far gone, not fully
lovely, changing each observer into architect?
To make posthistory wonder
what god needed a prosthesis
of compressed, freestanding steel. Monolith, a rock

band, fired igneous music through the bars
of Troy when I was seventeen. The dance floor weaved
with tawny light, a spectral
Navaho blanket. When the singer let me coil

wires into rings and figure eights
after the show, the place enlarged
to Madison Square Garden.

This was home: where girlish aspirations grew
flat as babies' heads
strapped into cradleboards, and boys
watched their hearts
like sundials that must remain unmoved
to point to something
true. What navigating fools

we were! We hadn't learned
a stable earthly object
kept on the left as referent
will send a traveler spiraling
into it, or that fixing on a heavenly body is the trick
to covering ground.
I read of others' sojourns
in the realms of gold and such
knowledge made me odd. Like a fig
grown in a Ripple bottle, my presence caused perplexity.

Leaving meant commencement.
Legend says an angel banished us
with a sword of flame, though rumor
claims the owners torched
our hangouts for insurance.
In any case, we preened with self-
congratulation, as though our origins were ruinous
accidents from which we'd walked away.

Fire fixes the magnetic alignment
of clay, and wooden beams remember
weather in their rings. But what Cortez will come
in search of tambourines and beads? We'd like a past
that won't decay with distance or yield
to interference. Failing that,
we want what we've abandoned
to wear: that is to crumble
and to last. We want a ruin: uselessness
permitted the luxury of existence.

When I returned, the shadow of a fire
escape—liquid, amenable
to every hive and crator—
engraved a devastation.
And foglamps, spiked and harsh,
bloomed like sunflowers crossed out with light.

Terrestrial Magnetism

Stars threatened you into feeling
negligible while susceptible
to connections, I saw many more
than two dippers riddling the sky.

Nights you'd leap down
from stellar atmospheres, wrap yourself
around me like a sari
as the lead guitar took his
solo. For the first time, I felt
singled out. I know you'd agree

that those letters written from faraway
gigs had the suspect sweetness of breath
mints, leaving me to guess what sour
moonlighting they covered,
and that losing you I lost

a language I couldn't stand
to have back, with words for need
obsessive as daylight,
a spectra glowing from all directions.

Together would we have fallen
into offices and sweated
under cubed light, would we
at day's end have gotten into better cars
than those we own and found without meaning
to we'd driven ourselves home?

I've spent years since
tracing the vapor formed between storm
and inner windows, sweeping the sky
for a star undigested by the dark, planet
perturbations, under the left breast, a heart.

News Of The Occluded Cyclone

Night usually computes itself in stars,
cryptic as a punchcard, but now the sky is blurry
as a turp-soaked rag.

At the siren we flip through frequencies
for the latest in tornado
warnings. We lose power and light

candles, their mild spices
comforting as cookies baking.
Thunder comes, galumphing its important

gavels. I wish it could call the storm
to an order arbitrary and dependable
as the ABCs. Instead, blackboards

embellished with unsteady
Y's are where
the windows used to be.

The sky is strung with lightning
like the lines of fighting
kites or tined with royal

racks that leave afterimages
of antlers on our sight.
We cling to each other

in the dead center of the living
room, as if the least space we can displace
is the one zoned for oasis, sensing as much

as seeing the dowsing
sticks above us. And it storms
till the candles form bright

putties in glass saucers, till the messy,
soft-edged dawn comes on
in rebuttal, and a voice disembodied

as God's proclaims the warning
over. There's a welcome
sense of excavation in the full-

frontal rush of morning, the horizon's
hierarchy under calm free-
falls of sun: it's deliverance

at a designated hour, this propriety
of day, this reliable frame
that lets color be

color and light light.

Where Are The Stars Pristine

Everyone's spending Christmas Eve adrift
in the corporal skirmish, mixing
up the darks with the lights, fending
with elbows and dirty
looks. Wet wool and down
crowd the air. Where are the stars, pristine
as great ideas? Behind clouds
the heavens saturate
with luminous dust, shuttles wearing halos
of earthdirt, light pollution
from jets fired to keep things
on course. Boys rickrack a ball off
floor and ceiling past the table
tree bubbling with giveaway
ornaments from Burger King and lights
that manage an occasional
lackadaisical flash. Showstoppers: everyone

looks every time and keeps looking
to make sure it happened.
The double frontloaders are going
like abstract TVs. And the program is important:
all about the boggling sullied
lives we'd like to hide.
But this is no place
to do so, where known
and unknown perverts come
to pirate underpants and the innocent
clutch their Cheer and Shout.

The rules are posted: only the toughest
habiliments, the superego
of raiment can take such agitation.
And only the poor are invited to endure
the sneezy powders and clean resentment.

Imagine a museum installation—
200 hypnotic washers stuffed with somersaulting
cloth. Critics could rise to the challenge,
their statements settling like coats
of gold and silver
chain mail over each machine:
"These Speed Queen pieces thrust ahead of art-
for-art's sake to confront us
with a realism of socio-political
magnitude. The vortex-like movement
of pattern, color, and texture infuses
these works with an abundance of unconscious
bliss. The soft forms
circulate with vigor
across the screens. The viewer
is not privy
to the cause of dirt
though one is witness to the dirt's
ablutions. The point is
we are not impeccable."

Everyone would be happy
to know that! And so we're forced to
scoop and pour
a fine white empathy over
the hairy flannels, snaggy nylons,
the glass front that gives
forth this light

industry, the silly tree
and jingles about blue and white
Christmases, chestnuts, sleighbells,
just as snow settles
on every unsequestered thing:

from blistered gum-
ball machines, clumsy bumpers,
crepuscular theaters with sticky floors,
to ramshackle mansions
choked with smiling
china animals where light shakes itself out
from TVs and old women
frail as walking sticks
sweep their stoops at eight a.m.
Just as snow makes the less than impeccable
classical, stroking the merely
drab or passing, quickly or slowly,
so we can count only on its
leaving, teaching
liquidity
to what seems solid.

Semaphores And Hemispheres

TO HANK

We take these days in the name of not-to-worry,
whether the sky appears carte blanche
or nerved with lightning
urgent as a breakdown,
whether we see cottages with curtains
neat as carded lace
or cedar shingles bleeding
into complicated grays. Whether our joy comes
unbidden, serendipitous—
a prince dropping a ring
into a stranger's cup—
or is created
the way clouds form
fortuitous crosses in 19th-century landscapes,

it's all the same to us. We arrived
to housing dank as a whale's
belly: a table made of pungent
stallboards, floors with holes
to lasso ankles, impastoed with oils
from artists not lost
but gone before, designer labels glued to each
appliance and a dead bass
in the Bill Blass broiler.
The roof leaked, of course,
so badly you rigged elaborate indoor gutters—
pipes, chains, buckets—and we had a sort of noisome
Italian water garden every time it rained.

In winter our pleasures were slim:
for an outing we'd joust the gale
on Commercial Street, watch the sun sink
into the bay like a pearl
dissolved in vinegar. We'd run
our numb fingers through the tide
of affordable unlikelies
at the Naval Supply (insect-obsessive
transistors, odd job lots
of somber cases for the purple heart, chaplain's
coats with crosses on the cuffs)
or gaze, fish-faced, at our reflections in the antique
periscopes. Often we'd see

a woman bareback on a springy Arab
by the Dairy Queen on Shankpainter,
mane flaggy, sienna
coat dappled as if containing
a hardly contained fire. Inside
the copy shop, attending to shades of gray,
I'd watch the horse move with earnest grace
on the dunes and wish for just that
wind-licking. I love the concept

of the gallop as a gait—
hooves striking ground quickly, even singly,
without a sign of tilt—the way I love
the sure angle of a lighthouse
beam that never bleeds into the night
but scrapes the black away to give the ocean back
its form, its body
that seems bellowed
by energies more ulterior than the moon's.

Whenever we visited the Highland Light
I couldn't keep up, in my tight fashion
jeans, as you ran waving
on the beach; the motion
of the lighthouse seemed closer, easier to read.
Back home, we meshed under the quilt's
tesserae of ancient clothes, under a patch
called Fly Foot or Catch-Me-
If-You-Can, hemstitches twining
an intaglio of trees, a semaphore
of roots and limbs that said your name and mine.

Eventually the sky decanted light, potable, giddy-
making as Pernod.
We saw people sipping
chowder with a side of cream,
and the smell of sugar-fried dough drifting
from the Portuguese Bakery lured us in
to drink a toast to spring.
Though coffee from the freshly scrubbed kitchen
rang of borax, we hardly cared.
All winter we'd listened to the anecdotal
elements, each with its story
of wear. After such severity, everything seemed rich

in metaphor: the crocuses poked up like palette
knives thick with yellow
oils, the pleasure
craft seemed moored by chains too glintingly
frivolous to hold such weight
by day; by dusk
their lights held them

above deckle-edged flirtatious waves.
If I'd learned anything I'd learned the sea
was easy to describe—call it formal
or amorphous, feeling or unfeeling—anything
eventually seems true. But no pains-
taking could copy its scrapyard
ad hoc, though we kept busy trying.

That day we found a buckskin
horse tethered in our neighbor's yard:
a grade animal, with its heavy stock
saddle beside it like a side of beef.
By circling in one direction it had wound itself
around a tree. Freeing it was like untangling
a 900-pound necklace, with all the lifting
of hooves and managing
of leads. It seemed both
imperturbable, interested only in its feed
and the whiff of distant equine, worthy
of the term "social
ungulate" from a textbook on domestic beasts,
and by virtue of its incongruity, a unicorn,
a steed with wingéd feet.

By Herring Cove we met a friend
who'd found the fossil of a cat's paw
mollusk, a cobble from the bottom
of an early sea. She said bivalves
form just enough shell to keep ahead
of body size. The one she held probably hobbled on one foot
less than 50 yards
in 50 years. Bits of shell
from its descendants are set
in oysters to get them to form

pearls. Then we saw the seals
swim close to shore, a wigwag
of neck-heads, like baby dinosaurs,
distant from us as seasons when the beach wavered
under erogenous sun, before the scene changed
like the moon, without entirely disappearing.
The ocean, too, forms

coigns more restless than the set
coigns of a crystal, and turbulence
in the air makes the stars
glimmer. Somehow
everything squares. The lighthouse oars the night
as if its white trunk could go soaring
up, concentric and outgoing
as a helicopter, unhurried
as a ceiling fan in old movies
of the tropics. And houses
on the cliff slip
in and out of dark
the way faces in a theater slip.
Consider our lives that make us
want to breathe
warnings, endearments, splendid
and banal as words before a voyage
on which all hands are lost.
Some days we're simply happy

to be just where we are,
where the lighthouse strokes
the hemispheres, a cane for the voyaging
blind, who chart their lives
by a star of the 19th magnitude
that shines unseen tonight but shines.

Traveling Light

Every restaurant boarded up in softwood,
bars strung with tipsy blinkers, smudgefires
against the dusk-
like day: who could have imagined the light
toppling down, song you can see
over all? Or this salt breeze,
vital and teary as a drunken wake.
The kite store's ringed with stunted Christmas
trees like pathetic closed umbrellas.
This is the year we'll trim with shells.
The man who sells them tells us tales
of smuggling, of price wars over apple coral,
fluted clams. His hair branches and his skin
hardens as he speaks: part baobab, part pirate.
His shells—little bandana prints, green turbans—
are lovely, "droll" might be the word,
but tropical, not from Cape Cod.

It was ten years ago this season
my father died, leaving me odd
wisdoms concerning clip joints,
gypsies, toeroom, elocution,
and traveling light. I was twenty,
up to my elbows in developer,
acid, fixative: a microfilm
technician with few discernible skills.
What would he have made of this off-season
resort? Though he never lived to see it
I can hear him say "Don't worry,

Al, if the poetry don't go
I'll buy you your own beauty shop."
Yes, with sickly pink
smells, well-thumbed back issues
of *Hairdo* and a 3-D religious picture
that flickered between Mary and Jesus,
in tricky light revealing
the Blessed Mother with a beard.
He liked scenery, Kay Francis
movies and the fights. I guess,
like you, I never really knew him.

On the last visit I ambled to his room
with my dignified mini hiked up
in the back, flashing
unintentional ass to the joyous
orderlies. Befuddled by dripping
liquids, screens yielding twitchy lights,
he said "What are we doing
in this carwash?" Then he thought he remembered
a long ago close call, when a canvas-topped jalopy
broke down in a Saratoga storm.
His hands froze first, then his flesh turned
dense as a snowman's. Only his brain kept
rolling. He knew he had no money.
The troopers took him to a sumptuous
hospital, and his eyes grew wondrous
as he raved and praised
the decor, the meals. "You can't imagine!
When I went to pay the nurses
said 'Mr. Fulton, it was a pleasure
to take care of you. There will be no charge.'"
There will be no charge

for the light or the sea's
skillful flippancies with it,
for the moon softening
the scene with its own
peculiar politeness.
After years of plea-bargaining
with a snooty muse, I've landed
here, where there's nothing I dread
doing. Gifts fall into my hands
from unindicted coconspirators; suddenly
all three Fates shine
their everloving light on me.
I'm free to watch the dunes
take on the chill
color of shells, the sea
threaten and beckon like a roof's edge,
an absentminded thing.
The way the tide rips itself
out sideways, thoughtless as a torn seam.

And people find things here I've heard:
Portuguese dolls, once encased in airy
pink and green crinolines swish in,
their mouths still
red and pouting. Here on the fragile tip
of this peninsula anything could
return. I'm half-prepared
for hostile mermaids, pilot whales, stranded
miscreants clad in moss and furs.
I'm half-prepared to see my father,
to whom the world gave nothing
without struggle, rise up beaming
anyway upon it, as if he never meant
to let it go. Saltboxes appear and disappear

in the slurry fog. Gulls open
against the sky like books
with blank, beautifully demanding pages,
and behind me the stolid ocean
slams itself on earth
as if to say *that's final*
though it isn't. Behind me the ocean
stares down the clouds, the little last remaining
light, as if to remind me of the nothing
I will always have
to fall back on.

ABOUT THE AUTHOR

Alice Fulton was born in Troy, New York, where she lived for twenty-five years. Her first book of poems, *Dance Script With Electric Ballerina,* won the 1982 Associated Writing Programs Award in poetry. She has published in *The New Yorker, The Yale Review, Poetry,* and *Parnassus,* among other magazines. Her honors include the 1980 Emily Dickinson Award and the 1984 Consuelo Ford Award from The Poetry Society of America. Alice Fulton has received fellowships from The Fine Arts Work Center in Provincetown, The Michigan Society of Fellows, and the John Simon Guggenheim Memorial Foundation. She is an assistant professor of English at the University of Michigan, Ann Arbor.